THE WEST KOOTENAY
IN PHOTOGRAPHS

Anne DeGrace & Steve Thornton
with David R. Gluns

Ward Creek Press

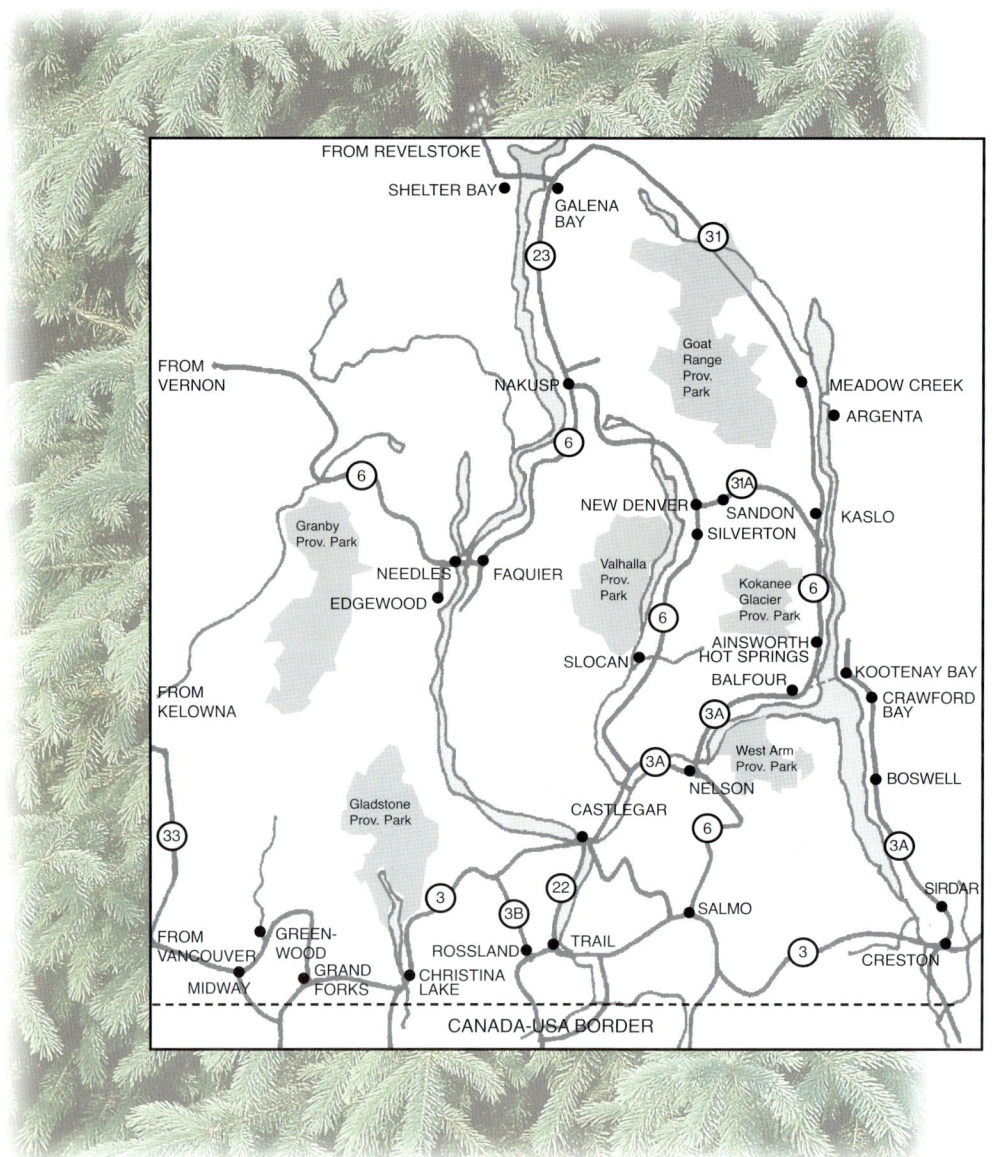

Ward Creek Press
1124 McQuarrie Ave.
Nelson, B.C. V1L 1B2
Ph/fax (250) 352-2026

Canadian Cataloguing in Publication Data

DeGrace, Anne
    The West Kootenay in Photographs

ISBN 0-9680739-1-3

    1. Kootenay Region (B.C.)—Pictorial works.
I. Thornton, Steve, 1950- II. Title

FC3849.K7D43 1997   971.1'62'0222   C97-900966-9
F1089.K7D43 1997

DeGrace, Anne and Thornton, Steve
The West Kootenay in Photographs

Cover photographs by David R. Gluns
Inside cover photograph by Jeremy Addington
Cover design by Fiona Richards, Silica Design
Production by Angela Lockerbie
Printed and bound in Canada by Friesens Printing

DAVID R. GLUNS

A ROCKY BEGINNING FOR A PLACE OF MARVELS

*F*irst, there was the dip of the paddle and the smell of wood smoke in a sparsely-peopled mountain country. Pictographs near *kootemik*, or "places of hot water," indicate that the soothing hot springs of the West Kootenay were revered thousands of years ago by British Columbia's first people. The Lower Kutenai and Lakes bands summered here, fishing the glacial rivers and lakes and hunting under forest cover. Then, late in the 19th Century, silver and gold were discovered in West Kootenay mountains and prospectors, fevered by dreams of instant riches, poured into the area.

Rossland's Sourdough Alley was probably the roughest and wildest thoroughfare in the province in 1895, a boomtown conflagration of tinhorns, prospectors, and prostitutes. With five newspapers, six churches, and 42 saloons, Rossland's 7,000 inhabitants were a well-informed and boisterous lot.

Fortunes were made, and sometimes lost. Fritz Augustus Heinze, who eventually founded a smelter at Trail, was a millionaire at 24. "Colonel" E.S. Topping purchased the famous LeRoi mine for $12.50, then sold it for $30,000. The propery eventually produced $40 million in rich ore. A squabble between Robert Sproule and Thomas Hammill over the Bluebell mine ended in murder. Characters like Cayuse Brown, Roughlock

Perry, Weary Willie, and The Yellow Kid came and went, leaving behind colourful scraps of history.

Rail and water were the highways of the time. The Kaslo & Slocan line covered treacherous terrain rising almost 600 metres (2,000 feet) to the famous Payne Bluff and its white-knuckle 330-metre drop. Kootenay and Arrow lakes' graceful sternwheelers, known as the "White Swans," carried ore from remote mining sites to railheads.

Catastrophes were not uncommon. Kaslo, Rossland, and Sandon each had its own "Great Fire," and Sandon, doubly unfortunate, was destroyed by a flood in 1955.

But it was a decline in resources that drew the curtain on this glittering, noisy heyday. As the dust settled, towns that looked toward logging and agriculture survived, and those depending on mining did not. Most of the overnight motherlodes of the 1880s had petered out within a few years: Sandon, Sheep Creek, Cody, Ferguson, Alamo, and Pilot Bay became ghost towns. Trail's Consolidated Mining and Smelting Company spelled that town's stability, while Nelson, Castlegar, Kaslo, and New Denver looked to forestry. Creston in the east, and Grand Forks in the west, found opportunities in agriculture.

Boom-and-bust cycles continued through West Kootenay towns during the early decades of the 20th Century. In 1942, there was a surprising influx of newcomers when thousands of dispossessed Japanese, torn

4

gone to weeds. Sandon is a historic site, some buildings restored to museums, others left to form a time-weathered backdrop. Nelson's restored buildings give it notability as a heritage centre. Ainsworth's J.B. Fletcher store now serves as a marketplace for West Kootenay artisans. Each town, from Grand Forks to Creston, from Salmo to Nakusp, celebrates its history through theatre, books and artworks, restored historic buildings, and museums.

But if the West Kootenay presents a window facing the past, it looks with growing acuity toward the future. Dependence on natural resources has often given way to such economic activities as tourism, technology, and the arts. Farming and logging—and to some extent, mining—remain vital, but diversification has strengthened the economy and immigration continues to bring new ideas.

There is tension, too, in concern about loss of life style. Opposition occasionally rears up against development. Battles are waged as environmentalists pit themselves against companies that cut and dig for resources. Natives, hunters, ranchers, and others struggle to make their voices heard as land-use decisions are hammered out. The area is evolving, physically, socially, and economically, and one can only hope the future is as generous as the past has been.

from their homes and businesses at the coast, were interned in Sandon, New Denver, Kaslo, Lemon Creek, and Greenwood. And as Japanese-Canadians wove their distinct thread into the fabric of West Kootenay communities, so, too, did the communal-living Doukhobors, dissenters from the Russian Orthodox Church who settled near Castlegar and Grand Forks around 1910.

Rustic reminders of past times are everywhere. Boaters find pictographs along shoreline rock faces, and scuba divers have discovered sunken maritime relics. Back roads reveal mine shafts and rusting equipment in the hillsides. Long-abandoned cabins hide in the trees, surrounded by the gnarled branches of orchards

Time will tell. But for the people here now, for those who come to visit, and for those who came before, the West Kootenay was and is a place of natural marvel, a place that stirs passions, and, like the hot waters of *kootemik*, soothes the spirit.

DAVID R. GLUNS

𝒜t the region's eastern border, Creston is the "gateway to the Kootenays," gracing a wide valley flanked by the Purcell and Selkirk mountains.

The textural patchwork of the Creston area is woven in the land. Fruit orchards and hayfields nudge cow pastures and berry plantations to form an agricultural mosaic. The reclamation of some 10,000 hectares (25,000 acres) of land from the floodwaters of the Kootenay River spawned the Creston Flats, and with that a reputation as the West Kootenay's prime growing area.

𝒫icking season is a source of seasonal employment that draws locals and outsiders alike into the tidy rows of well-laden fruit trees. Roadside fruit stands afford an opportunity to buy fresh-picked fruit from the source.

DAVID R. GLUNS

6

Creston is an agricultural community, but like many West Kootenay towns, has looked increasingly to tourism. With an opening of doors comes community pride, and to this end Creston has worked to beautify its downtown core with a series of murals that reflect the history and the land. Events such as the annual Blossom Festival in May serve as both community celebration and visitor attraction. A downtown artisans' collective reflects a large artistic community riding on the coattails of the tourism wave.

DAVID R. GLUNS

DAVID R. GLUNS

*S*een from above (facing page), the sanctuary is a soft green paradise of islands floating in a bluesky stream.

LINDA VAN DAMME

*B*irdsong echoes through the wetland environments of the Kootenay River (above), and the Creston Valley Wildlife Management Area, which holds 6,800 hectares (17,000 acres) of wetland. At least 250 species of birds make their homes in this protected area.

DAVID R. GLUNS

*G*lorious lake-and-mountain vistas greet the eye at nearly every turn of Highway 3A as it unfolds along the east shore of Kootenay Lake, where cosy hamlets like Riondel, Crawford Bay, Boswell, and Kuskonook embrace the sparkling natural scenery. Along one of the most enjoyable drives in the West Kootenay area, the Sirdar Pub north of Creston is a favourite pitstop.

*T*he Glass House (above) is the final resting place of 500,000 embalming fluid bottles, a project begun in 1952 by retired funeral home director David H. Brown. The house design, a clover-leaf uniting three circular rooms, is as unusual as the materials.

Turning an avocation into a small industry, Kootenay Forge owner John Smith tried his hand at blacksmithing in Nova Scotia while earning his living as a farmer. He moved to B.C. in the early '80s and set up a forge at Crawford Bay, where with a team of blacksmiths he turns out decorative and functional ironworks. Some of the tools in his shop date back to the turn of the century.

Cottage industry finds a comfortable home on the East Shore--just down the road are The Weaver's Corner and The North Woven Broom Company.

STEVE THORNTON

DAVID R. GLUNS

DAVID R. GLUNS

*O*perating year-round, the *Anscomb* and the *Balfour* carry passengers across Kootenay Lake--a free ferry ride enhanced by panoramic shorescape views.

*N*atural hot springs are reminders of more geologically active times, when a tectonic smooch far below opened fissures to lakes of superheated water. Ainsworth Hot Springs (right) is a full-featured tourist attraction, but others remain *au naturel*.

GORDON F. BROWN

DAVID R. GLUNS

Nature's moods are no less important in a village where winter can mean a telemark turn through the snow before heading home to chop more firewood, and summer, a bone-chilling splash in glacier-fed Kootenay Lake after a hot day at the jazz festival.

A village where loggers and logging protestors may share elbow-space at the local watering hole after a day in the woods, Kaslo is enlivened by the diverse ideologies of its inhabitants. Residents maintain an intense interest in community affairs, engaging in heated debates in the village hall and relaxed cracker-barreling outside the Mystic Convenience Store.

GORDON F. BROWN

14

The Langham (right), a Kaslo landmark, was a rooming house for miners in the late 1800s. Fifty years ago, Japanese-Canadians were interned here, and a display memorializes that period. Today, it's a museum, gallery, and theatre—a bastion of culture for the region.

Rooftops afford a bird's-eye view for Kaslo townsfolk gathered for the Mayday parade, the hub of an annual festival that began in 1893.

DAVID R. GLUNS

DAVID R. GLUNS

DAVID R. GLUNS

$\mathcal{A}$ welcome sign greets arrivals to Argenta at the north end of Kootenay Lake. Isolated and largely agrarian, the small community is home to Quakers ("Friends"), who emigrated from California in 1952, and others who appreciate country living. Rhonda Gates (right) displays a barrow of fresh carrots in front of her bed-and-breakfast home, one of the settlement's few tourist accommodations.

$\mathcal{C}$lear, blue, and cold, the waters of Poplar Lakes (facing page) reflect the sky over Goat Range Provincial Park in the Selkirk mountains between Argenta and Nakusp.

18

A classic boom-and-bust tale describes the history of Sandon, a ghost town located in a narrow valley between New Denver and Kaslo. Choked with prospectors and miners in the 1890s, the village was a banker's (or gambler's) dream come true. As mineral resources dwindled, the people left, and by the '30s Sandon was an empty shell. Repopulated a few years later by Japanese-Canadians forced there by a wartime government, the village echoed briefly to the sounds of restrained life, but in 1955 an aging flume built to contain the creek that ran beneath Sandon's main street became jammed with logs, and the ensuing washout destroyed the village.

Today, the Sandon Historical Society maintains the area and buildings, including a visitors' centre, museum, and café. Although restoration is underway on some buildings, many appear unvisited by humans since the heyday of miners and prospectors.

Craggy mountains set a dramatic backdrop (facing page) for trail riders near Kokanee Glacier Park in the Enterprise Creek drainage area.

DAVID R. GLUNS

DAVID R. GLUNS

DAVID R. GLUNS

DAVID R. GLUNS

*S*mall-town charm need not be without culture. The Silverton Gallery hosts exhibitions of visual art, performances, and literary readings. Valley Best, an annual event show-casing locally-produced works, pulls rural artists from their forest garrets to fill walls and plinths with all manner of creative enterprise.

*S*ilverton Resort (facing page), one of many area retreats which offer respite from life's pres-sures, is the first sight to greet road travelers heading north into the village.

DAVID R. GLUNS

DAVID R. GLUNS

*W*inding, sparsely-trafficked roads are a motorcyclist's delight. Idaho Peak (right, and facing page), offers one of the best views in the West Kootenay. The trail to the lookout starts at 2,150 metres (7,000 feet), but is worth the legwork.

23

*C*afés serve as meeting places for small-town residents and their rural neighbours. In New Denver, octogenarian John Oxley, a former village mayor, is such a regular at the Appletree Restaurant that he has his own key—so he can get the java brewing early. Just up the street, the Silver Spoon offers the fragrance of fresh-baked pastries to lure passersby.

DAVID R. GLUNS

PATRIZIA MENTON

24

A clapboard cabin, built in 1942 to house Japanese-Canadians expelled from coastal homes, is part of the Nikkei Internment Memorial Centre in New Denver. An important link to the past, the centre reconstructs a wartime internment community called "the Orchard," and is nearly all that remains from that period. While most Japanese were forced out of British Columbia in a second massive expulsion after the war, some were allowed to stay, among them Tad Mori (inset), who remembers that New Denver neighbours treated the internees with a measure of kindness.

A story of loss, shattered communities, and rebirth, the Nikkei centre provides a glimpse of what life was like in hard times.

STEVE THORNTON

A product of the Slocan silver rush, Nakusp established itself on the hospitable shores of Upper Arrow Lake 100 years ago. With good farmland and an abundance of surrounding timber, the village prospered, using paddle wheelers and steam tugs to transport goods to markets through the first half of the century.

*T*oday, forestry shares the economic tableau with tourism, and though the paddle wheels are gone, pleasure boats share the lake with a large and vigorous osprey population.

DAVID R. GLUNS

DAVID R. GLUNS

$\mathcal{E}$vening is a peaceful time on West Kootenay waterfronts. A healthy catch of fish is a happy reward after a day on the water.

$\mathcal{F}$ading light wraps Nakusp's marina in soft tranquility (facing page).

The village is a doorway to a large water system that reaches north to Revelstoke, and south, by way of Lower Arrow Lake, to Castlegar. The communities of Burton, Fauquier, Needles, and Edgewood, near the centre of the north-south reach of the two lakes, lie close to a stretch of highway that runs over the Monashee mountains and connects the area with the Okanagan Valley.

DAVID R. GLUNS

*F*ormed in the valleys between mountain ranges and fed by melting snow, the long, narrow Arrow Lakes are typical of West Kootenay waterways. An aerial view reveals the landscape—a mirror-flat surface below a wave of craggy, snow-capped mountains.

*F*oot up and coffee mug handy, an Arrow Lakes ferry captain keeps an eye on his ship's course as he steers toward Galena Bay, bringing vehicles and people into West Kootenay country from Revelstoke and the Trans-Canada Highway.

DAVID R. GLUNS

Plop! A trout's leap momentarily craters the surface of Upper Arrow Lake as evening falls, windless and warm. The ruby rays of a descendent sun illuminate boaters and a fish that took the bait. West Kootenay lakes and streams hold a variety of sport fish, notably kokanee, rainbow trout, Dolly Varden char, and bull trout.

*K*okanee Glacier Park (following page) rewards adventurous hikers with scenes of exquisite beauty. Valhalla Provincial Park's breathtaking wilderness lies west of Slocan Lake (page 33).

DAVID R. GLUNS

DAVID R. GLUNS

LARRY DOELL

*H*ighway and river run side-by-side through the Slocan Valley, where farming and logging sustain many residents. The mill at Slocan City (it's actually a village) is of major economic importance, while small business, education, and other forms of employment also contribute.

*S*now falls around loggers where a patch of forest has been clear cut. There is disagreement about the effects of this type of logging, but it pays the bills for many Kootenay residents.

Galleries are a ubiquitous roadside attraction in the West Kootenay, testament to a large artistic community that thrives on the peace found in a rural lifestyle. A Place in the Forest is a tiny gallery tucked among the pines near Winlaw.

ANNE DEGRACE

Snow melt means flood waters in the spring, compromising livestock and, occasionally, human dwellings. Dam systems offer some control, but residents watch river banks closely as the weather warms.

PHIL HARRISON

35

DAVID R. GLUNS

*W*ith a melody in the air and coins in his case, a busker works the sidewalk on Nelson's Baker Street.

A parade float celebrates the red-white-and-green flag of Italy and the contributions of Italian traditions to the city of Nelson. Drawn by mining and rail employment opportunities late in the 19th Century, Italian-Canadians settled in several West Kootenay towns, including Rossland and Trail.

*K*eeping up appearances (right) a painter restores a downtown building front.

LARRY DOELL

DAVID R. GLUNS

Nelson residents exhibit pride in their gardens, often embracing a look at once cultivated and wild. The city's accent on tourism has led to a proliferation of bed-and-breakfast establishments which offer the warmth of personal contact along with well-tended grounds and a relaxed ambience. Tastefully restored downtown heritage buildings, enjoyed by many, have benefited from government revitalization programs and community enthusiasm.

JEREMY ADDINGTON

DAVID R. GLUNS

An initiative of the last decade, stone murals on the walls of village buildings were projects of students attending the nearby Kootenay Stone Training Institute. Mining history and area wildlife are predominant themes.

DAVID R. GLUNS

Salmo, Ymir, and Erie began almost simultaneously in the 1890s, springing to life with ore discoveries and settled strategically along the right-of-way of the historic Nelson-Fort Shepherd Railway. Ymir ("why-mir"), by far the largest and most prosperous at the turn of the century, has diminished in size since the mines became silent, and Erie has almost entirely vanished. Salmo held on, and today owes much to its location at the junction of two highways and the determined efforts of its citizens to enhance their community.

40

PHIL HARRISON

STEVE THORNTON

LARRY DOELL

The highway bridge at Taghum, just west of Nelson, parallels an older railway line crossing the Kootenay River. A shoreline farm (above) is a scene of quiet, misty beauty as the morning sun warms the waters. This stretch of the river passes over a series of dams, where hydro-electric power is generated to supply local needs.

PHIL HARRISON

*A*t the meeting place of the Kootenay and Columbia rivers sits Castlegar, which found its beginnings in the convergence of railway lines that linked the Columbia, Kootenay, and Western routes and earned it the handle, "the Crossroads of the Kootenays."

*B*etween 1908 and 1913, some 5,000 Doukhobors came to Ootischenia (the Valley of Consolation) near Castlegar. Originally Russian emigrés, they sought a place where they could live according to their religious principles, and in Ootischenia's fertile soil planted the seeds of a strong cultural community.

*O*verlooking the city of Castlegar, the Doukhobor Historical Village museum (right) traces the early communal life of this group, which espoused a maxim of "toil and a peaceful life."

DAVID R. GLUNS

43

The new Celgar Pulp Mill at Castlegar, a $700 million project, is one of the area's largest employers and is head-and-shoulders cleaner than the old mill, which was started in 1960 and employed what one expert called "rudimentary" pollution controls. About $100 million went into making the new mill a safer producer, so discharges into the Columbia River and emissions into the air are greatly reduced. Celgar produces 400,000 tonnes of pulp each year.

The city of Castlegar and the Columbia River (facing page) are rendered in pastel shades by a West Kootenay twilight.

DAVID R. GLUNS

LARRY DOELL

The city of Trail on a winter evening (facing page) shines brightly, casting colourful reflections on the Columbia River.

A quiet morning is reflected in a Trail bookstore (below). St. Anthony's Catholic Church (right) lies at the foot of a historic area called "the Gulch," a patchwork of steeply-climbing streets and older family homes where many Italian-Canadians live. Trail has the greatest concentration of Italians in North America, many of whom congregate at St. Anthony's.

STEVE THORNTON

ANNE DEGRACE

47

Cominco's smokestack towers over a downtown street in Trail. While the city's skyline is dominated by the giant smelter, Trail is architecturally and structurally beautiful, climbing hillsides from the banks of the Columbia River and employing brick and stone materials in classic building designs. The city was founded in 1901 as a smelter site for Rossland's prolific gold mine, but while Rossland eventually languished under diminished mining activity, Trail and Cominco flourished. It's not a company town any longer, though many residents still work at the smelter operation; companies and workers that once relied solely on Cominco have turned outward, penetrating markets around the world.

Picturesque, quaint, some even say cartoon-like, the village of Warfield (facing page) has been called "Mickey Mouse Town" because the small, steeply-roofed houses built before World War II looked as if they might have been drawn for an animated film. Nestled between Trail and Rossland, this community is the very essence of small-town, family living.

LARRY DOELL

*S*kiing is a popular winter pastime at Rossland, which boasts some of the finest slopes and cross-country trails in British Columbia.

*R*ossland displays a fairy-tale setting in winter twilight. After a frosty day skiing Red Mountain's Powder Field or traversing the back country, it's a warming sight to come upon the lights of the village, where a crackling fire and a good meal await.

LARRY DOELL

*H*er rosy spire a village landmark, St. Andrew's United Church overlooks a downtown setting that brims with appealing touches. Hundred-year-old buildings bedecked with bright awnings and colourful trim, set against a mountain backdrop, make Rossland a scene of considerable charm. A walk down Columbia Avenue on a sunny day can take a while, involving comfortable curbside chats or neighbourly cups of coffee at a local bistro.

*S*ituated 1,000 metres (3,400 feet) above sea level, Rossland often finds itself aswirl in snowflakes come winter's winds, but summer brings warmth and plenty of sunshine to this "Alpine City." Though very close to Trail, the community is distinctive, with design guidelines guarding architectural integrity and an economy strengthened by a growing number of smart, small businesses.

LARRY DOELL

51

In 1890 prospector Joe Moris staked five claims on Red Mountain, and soon people were calling the town "the Golden City." Within a few years it was a sophisticated boomtown, its saloons offset culturally with the International Music Hall and the Opera House and professionally with 17 law firms. Despite the heady smell of gold in the air, the Rossland branch of the Western Federation of Miners was instrumental in ensuring the adoption of legislation concerning the eight-hour work day and workers' compensation. The restored Miner's Union Hall, built by the federation in 1898, is the last remaining in Canada.

A canoe glides over a marbled green river bottom as two paddlers enjoy a popular West Kootenay activity. With an abundance of lakes, rivers, and streams, the area offers waterways for canoeists and kayakers of all skill levels, who indulge in everything from charging down a whitewater gauntlet to dozing on an inner tube along a sleepy river.

*W*ater lilies decorate the quiet inlets of Nancy Greene Lake, a short distance north of Rossland in the Monashee mountains. The lake and surrounding Nancy Greene Provincial Park, opened in 1972, are ideal for such activities as fishing, camping, cross-country skiing, and even—with occasional windy conditions—wind surfing.

53

DAVID R. GLUNS

DAVID R. GLUNS

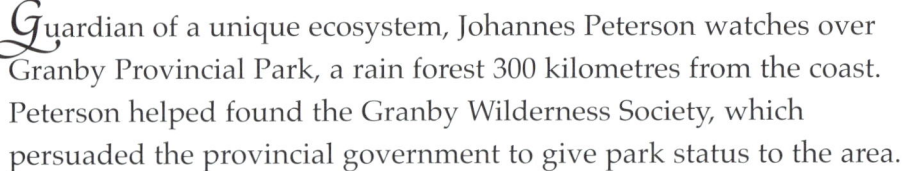

EVA ANTHONY

Guardian of a unique ecosystem, Johannes Peterson watches over Granby Provincial Park, a rain forest 300 kilometres from the coast. Peterson helped found the Granby Wilderness Society, which persuaded the provincial government to give park status to the area.

A young couple and their dog relax by the Granby River, while a coyote surveys its leafy domain. The West Kootenay is home to an abundance of wildlife. Grizzly and black bear, wolverine, cougar, moose, and many other species inhabit the region.

54

*C*atching a wave in her little blue bucket, a young visitor enjoys the waters of Christina Lake, one of the country's warmest. A mecca for vacationers, the lake was established as a holiday destination in the 1940s and is rimmed by cottages. The village of the same name (taken from the daughter of a Hudson's Bay trader of the mid-1800s) thrives on a summer tourist trade but is home to a number of year-round residents.

DAVID R. GLUNS

LARRY DOELL

$\mathcal{S}$waybacked shack confronts the arid environs of Grand Forks hill country (facing page), where the Okanagan Valley brushes up against the wetter Kootenays.

$\mathcal{A}$ horse and aging but still-pretty barn are signs of a thriving farming community, while (right) fields are kept green by generous watering when the hills behind them suffer the parching effects of a long, hot summer.

STEVE THORNTON

DAVID R. GLUNS

VICKI HART

$\mathcal{L}$ike other West Kootenay communities, Grand Forks carries a history rich in mining and agricultural enterprise. Today, the fertile land around the city, bathed in sunshine for much of the year, yields a variety of crops, including potatoes, berries, and flowers. Doukhobors settled in the area decades ago, and their characteristically square, brick dwellings dot the landscape (facing page).

$\mathcal{D}$owntown Grand Forks reflects the pride of an old city and the relaxed demeanour of a small town, where you can lounge outside a shop with a good book or take in the sights, which include the restored post office, currently serving as city hall.

DAVID R. GLUNS

The saloon at Greenwood is a historical landmark still enjoyed by locals and tourists. The nation's smallest city, Greenwood lies in the middle of Boundary country, where the West Kootenay meets the Okanagan Valley.

Mountain bikers (facing page) enjoy a pause near Midway, the oldest townsite in the Boundary region. Positioned halfway between the Rocky Mountains and the Pacific Ocean, Midway is one of the most westerly communities in the West Kootenay region. The Kettle River Museum keeps the area's history alive and celebrates the Kettle Valley Railway, which hazarded extremely difficult terrain and became the most expensive rail line ever laid. Abandoned years ago, the KVR rail bed has been recycled for two-wheeled users and is part of an extensive network of recreational trails.

DAVID R. GLUNS

A lake glimmers in late afternoon sunlight, a mountain range is softly illuminated by a setting sun—these images remain in the memory of anyone who has ever traveled through the West Kootenay. But other memories linger, too. The sound of a fish leaping in a calm pond, the smell of new growth in an April forest, the sight of lovingly restored buildings in a town full of history— all these things, and more, make up the West Kootenay. So diverse is this region that to experience all of it would require a lifetime—but to have experienced any of it, no matter how briefly, is surely to have enriched a life.

DAVID R. GLUNS

DAVID R. GLUNS

PRINCIPAL PHOTOGRAPHER: David R. Gluns

CONTRIBUTING PHOTOGRAPHERS: Jeremy Addington, Eva Anthony, Gordon F. Brown, Anne DeGrace, Larry Doell, Barney Gilmour, Phil Harrison, Vicki Hart, Patrizia Menton, Steve Thornton, Linda Van Damme.

ACKNOWLEDGEMENTS

This book would not have been possible without the kind participation of many West Kootenay residents. To those who endured our questions and patiently explained the facts, who allowed photographers onto their property and gracefully permitted cameras to be turned their way, and who provided advice and encouragement, our thanks. Especially deserving of mention are Verna Relkoff and Shawn Lamb, whose assistance saved the authors some embarrassment and provided the text much improvement.